REPTILES OF THE WORLD FUN FACTS FOR KIDS

SPEEDY
PUBLISHING

Speedy Publishing LLC
40 E. Main St. #1156
Newark, DE 19711
www.speedypublishing.com

Copyright 2015

Reptiles are a group of animals comprising today's turtles, crocodilians, snakes, lizards, tuatara, and their extinct relatives.

There are more than 8,000 species of reptiles on the planet. Reptiles are among the longest-lived species on the planet.

Reptiles are covered in scales or have a bony external plate such as a shell. Reptiles do not have sweat or sebaceous glands.

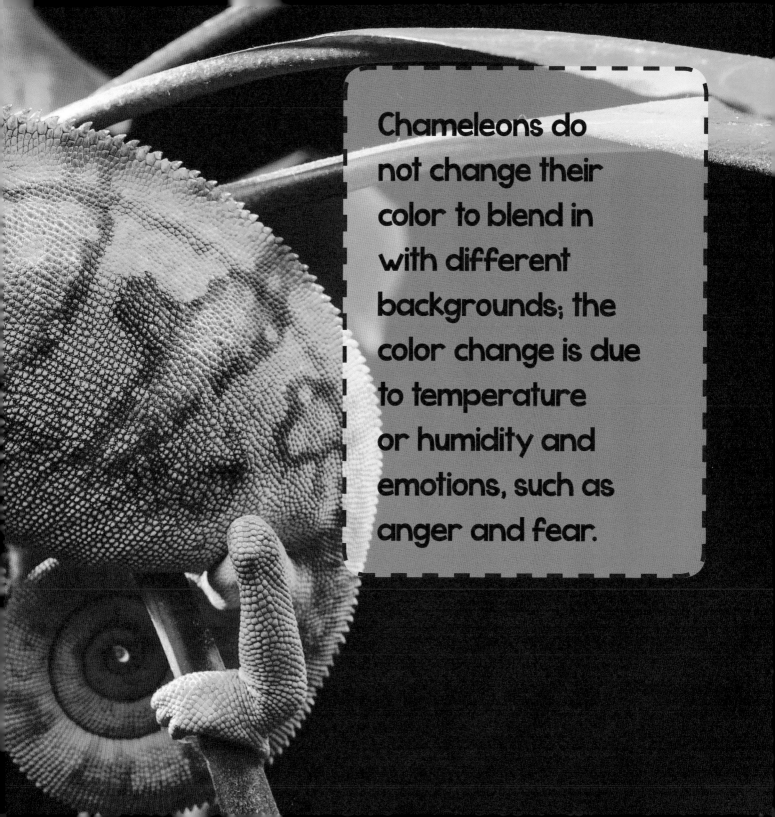

Chameleons do not change their color to blend in with different backgrounds; the color change is due to temperature or humidity and emotions, such as anger and fear.

Reptiles are cold-blooded animals, which means that they depend on external sources to maintain their body temperatures.

Reptiles are thought to have evolved about 340 million years ago from a group of reptile-like amphibians called the Reptiliomorphs.

Reptiles are tetrapods which means they have 4 limbs. Although snakes have lost their legs during the course of evolution, they are tetrapods by descent.

Reptiles can be found
on every continent
except for Antarctica.

Printed in Great Britain
by Amazon